That is why it was called Babel—because there the LORD confused the language of the whole world. From there the LORD scattered them over the face of the whole earth. (Genesis 11:9, NIV[1])

After this I looked and there before me was a great multitude that no one could count, from every nation, tribe, people and language, standing before the throne and in front of the Lamb. They were wearing white robes and were holding palm branches in their hands. (Revelation 7:9)

INTRODUCTION

Babel's effects continue, and not only among modern "tower builders." Misunderstandings related to the nature of language also confuse the Church, whether in missionary work, cross-cultural dialogue or the use of the Bible itself. Sadly, there is a great deal of babble spread around concerning the essence of Bible translation. Intra-church strife, and even carnage, result from Babel's confusion. This work, drawn upon the study of numerous languages and cultures, is an attempt to dispel some of that confusion.

1. THE BIBLE IN HISTORY

The ability to read and write may well be the most important achievement of humanity. Of all that has ever been written, without a doubt the Bible is the most influential. It has shaped lives, languages, cultures, societies and entire epochs.

The Bible began over three thousand years ago with an insignificant people, the Hebrews. Miraculously, their descendants, language, culture and Book are still with us today. That Book spread to the Greeks through the Septuagint, a translation begun in the 3rd century B.C. The real Author of the Book then visited earth in human form. The world has never been the same. The Author's writings were expanded (we call it the "New Testament"), completed, and translated into Latin, Syriac, Coptic, Gothic, Ethiopic, Armenian and Georgian. The truths of the heavenly Book conquered the earth's Roman conquerors. After serving as the basis of Islam—although in a regrettably altered form—the Book flowed north to the Slavs and later, during the time of the Reformation, leaped throughout the major languages of Western Europe. The modern Bible translation movement, begun by William Carey in India, has encompassed the globe.

Currently, at least a portion of the translated Scriptures exists in more than two thousand languages, spoken by over ninety percent of the world's population. Translation of the Bible continues in more than a thousand languages, and even in those languages where it has long been in existence, new translations continue to be made.

"The kingdom of heaven is like a mustard seed ... Though it is the smallest of all your seeds, yet when it grows, it is the largest of garden plants and becomes a tree, so that the birds of the air come and perch in its branches." (Matthew 13:31-32)

BIBLE, BABEL AND BABBLE

THE FOUNDATIONS OF BIBLE TRANSLATION

SCOTT MUNGER

2. COMMON MISCONCEPTIONS ABOUT BIBLE TRANSLATION

Fiction: ***If you need to sleep, try translation.***
Fact: If you translate the Bible, you may lose sleep. The responsibility is huge, and the pressures—religious, governmental, administrative, satanic—can be daunting.

Fiction: ***Those who have a dictionary can translate the Bible.***
Fact: Generally speaking, the more focus on a dictionary, the less focus on context, reader comprehension and the actual meaning. Training is vital. Translators must juggle not only languages, but cultures, religions and political climates. They also need an understanding of semantics, biblical studies, archeology, sociolinguistics and computers.

Fiction: ***The more letters after a person's name, the less help he or she needs.***
Fact: Highly educated people have more than once produced a poor translation. "He who stands, take heed lest he fall."

Fiction: ***The more "idiomatic" or "dynamic" a translation, the easier it is to do.***
Fact: The more literal a translation, the easier it is to do (but the harder it is to understand). "Contemporary" translations have the irksome tendency of saying wrong things in an attractive way. Only great care and checking can avoid this pitfall.

Fiction: ***Translating is like harvesting grain with a scissors—one stalk at a time.***

Fact: Translation is more like clearing a mountainside covered not only with grass, but also shrubs, trees and rocks. It addition to words, phrases and verses, the rugged terrain of translation includes paragraphs, sections, chapters and truths found elsewhere in the Bible.

Fiction: ***Translation is a lonely job, done amidst dusty old tomes.***

Fact: Translation is done with people. Reference books contain many riches, but a translation is meant to communicate. So translators need time with people, testing the text to see if it is clear and powerful. They should cultivate relationships with the "gatekeepers." Finally, they must love their audience, for only then can they consistently make God's thoughts clear.

Fiction: ***Bible translators merely translate.***

Fact: Bible translators are:
- Farmers, making "food" for the world.
- Journalists, giving access to vital information.
- Revolutionaries, overthrowing falsehoods.
- Church planters, laying a foundation for the Church.
- Entertainers, telling the greatest story ever.
- Soldiers, protecting the defenseless and invading Satan's territory.
- Economists, helping people manage life's real resources.
- Transporters, moving people from one kingdom to another.

Fiction: ***The translator's goal is to publish a book.***

Fact: The translator's goal is to change lives, cultures and societies—to change eternity on a grand scale. Things don't get much bigger than that.

3. WHAT IS TRANSLATION?

The English word "translate" comes from the Latin *translatus*, meaning "to bear/carry/bring across; to transfer." When referring to language, it is only fair to ask what is carried across, what is transferred? Ultimately, there can only be one answer:

M E A N I N G

The fundamental distinction between "meaning" and "form" must always be clear in the mind of a translator. Meaning is the idea, sense, thought or message; form is the structure used to convey it from one person to another. Form may be written or spoken, seen or heard. It is built from such familiar elements as sounds, letters, words and what is commonly called "grammar." Form is variable, meaning is not. Form is the wrapper, meaning is the food it contains; form is the suitcase, meaning is its contents; form is the body, meaning is the soul. Meaning is transferred by forms but is almost always distinct from them.

This can be demonstrated by two parallel truths, namely: 1) meaning may be expressed by different forms; 2) a single form may express different meanings. The vast diversity between languages clearly supports the first of these, but even one language can express an idea by several different forms:

> They blamed John for the problem.
> They blamed the problem on John.
> They said John was responsible for the problem.
> They accused John of being responsible for the problem.
> (Adapted from an example by Ken Pike.)

Likewise, a single form may express several different meanings. Note the following set of identical forms where a noun + possessive (e.g., *David + 's*) is followed by another noun.

FORM	MEANING	RE-EXPRESSION
(noun + 's + noun)		
{ sword }	ownership	"the sword David owned"
{ song }	authorship	"the song David wrote"
David's { son }	kinship	"the son David begot"
{ city }	domicile/rule	"the city where David lived"
{ sin }	action	"the sin David committed"

In each case the grammatical form is the same, yet each time an entirely distinct meaning is conveyed by that form. Note the additional example below where the same Greek phrase or "form"—ἀγάπη τοῦ θεοῦ (*agapē tou theou*)—has two very different meanings.

- Romans 8:39   =   "God loves us"   ("love of God")
- 1 John 5:3   =   "We love God"   ("love for God")

Clearly, form is distinct from meaning.

4. THE TRANSLATION PROCESS

Once the distinction between form and meaning is clear, a definition of translation can be given: Translation is a two-step process by which meaning expressed in the form of one language is re-expressed in the form of another. Schematically, this can be shown as follows (adapted from Larson[2]):

Linguistic Form of Source Language

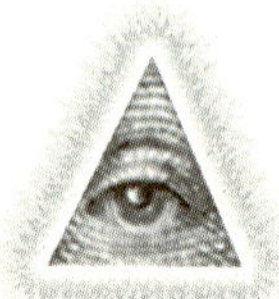

Meaning

Linguistic Form of Receptor Language

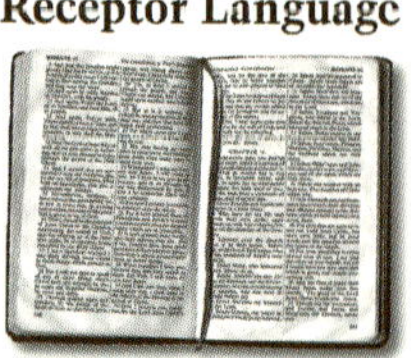

Step 1 is to discover or clarify the meaning of the source language text (in the field of biblical studies this is often called "exegesis"). Step 2 is to re-express that meaning in forms natural to the receptor language. We see, therefore, that translation first and foremost is a transfer of meaning. Whereas the form of the receptor language will differ from that of the source language, the meaning should remain constant.

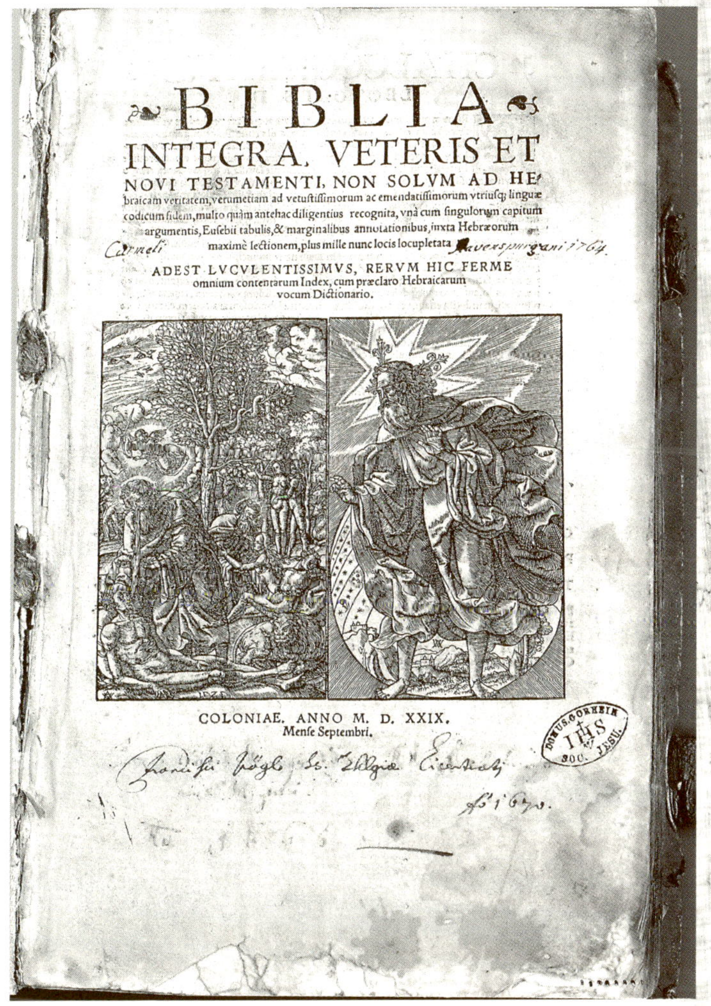

5. TRANSLATION AND THE BIBLE

The following five truths move us logically from the discussion above, where translation is presented in theory, to its actual practice as applied to the Bible.

- It is impossible to translate the Bible literally without loss or confusion of meaning.
- The Bible itself gives examples of meaning-based translation.
- The Bible does not teach literal translation.
- The Church fathers do not teach literal translation.
- For most audiences, the goal is an accurate yet clear and natural-sounding translation.

Each of these truths will be looked at in turn.

5.1 It Is Impossible to Translate the Bible Literally Without Loss or Confusion of Meaning

Take, for instance, an example from English into Russian: "The boy threw the ball." Since Russian does not have articles ("the" or "a"), it is impossible to translate this sentence literally. The closest one can come is: Мальчик бросил мяч (*Mal'chik brosil myach*). Translated back into literal English this would be "Boy threw ball." The Russian sentence on its own is ambiguous. It could mean:

- "A boy threw a ball,"
- "The boy threw a ball,"
- "The boy threw the ball," or,
- "A boy threw the ball."

Only by context can one tell what the Russian means. The English form, however, implies that a specific boy and a specific ball are part of the known

context. The question then arises, can meaning be transferred from English into Russian? Certainly. By introducing the context—the boy and the ball, both of which are assumed by the use of "the" in the original English sentence—the Russian sentence is then specific:

Был/есть мальчик с мячом. Мальчик бросил мяч. *Byl/yest' mal'chik s myachom. Mal'chik brosil myach.*

Translated back into English this becomes, "There was/is a boy with a ball. ['The'—now understood from the context] boy threw ['the'—also understood from the context] ball."

So we see that it is possible to transfer the meaning, but it is impossible to do so by translating the English sentence literally into Russian.

Among the thousands of examples that could be drawn from the Bible itself, a verse that clearly illustrates this point is 1 Peter 1:10. The rendering found in the *King James Version* (*KJV*) is quite literal:

> Of which salvation the prophets have inquired and searched diligently, who prophesied of the grace *that should come* unto you.

But even here, not only did the translators add the words in italics ("that should come"), they changed the entire structure of the text. Compare the *KJV* translation, above, with the rendering below, which more closely follows the actual Greek text:

> Around which salvation out-sought and out-studied prophets the around the for you grace prophesying-ones ...

What sense can be made of that?! It might mean something to someone who is fluent in both Greek and English, but not to a person who only knows the latter. Like it or not, those who want a truly literal translation should abandon their hope. Even the most literal of versions is not entirely literal, since the words and expressions of languages never completely overlap. Thoughts and ideas are essentially identical, regardless of the language. But it is the almost limitless variety of forms (sounds, words, grammar, etc.) that distinguish one language from another, and it is the forms that must change during the proper translation of thoughts. Those who refuse to recognize the need for such changes in form— those who want the *words*

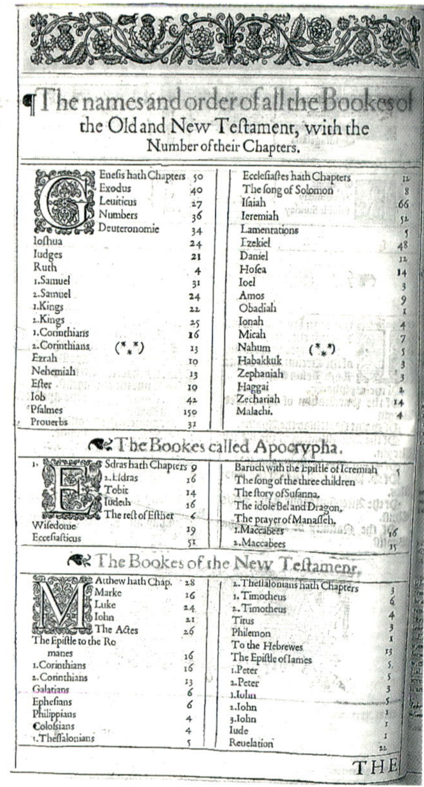

to precisely follow the original—should read only the original language text, or else read nothing at all.

Objections are often expressed against anything other than a word-for-word, "literal" translation. A proponent of the exclusive use of the *KJV* has written:

> ... what about our belief in verbal inspiration? If it's only the "thought" that counts, then the words are flexible, and we can adjust them to make them convey any thought we prefer. Exact thoughts require precise words.[3]

In response, first of all, it should be noted that this is self-contradictory. If it is truly "the 'thought' that counts," then translators obviously do **not** have the right to "convey any thought [they] prefer." On the contrary, they dare only convey the thought of the original writer!

Second, while it is true that to convey thoughts properly requires "precise words," a vital question remains: What words? The only answer can be "The words of the language into which the original is being translated." As anyone who speaks more than one language knows, there is obviously no word-for-word correspondence between languages. For that reason, no translator who wants to communicate meaning to a typical audience should follow a word-for-word paradigm, whether in theory or practice.

SALM XXIII.

Hyder Dafydd ar ras Duw.

¶ Salm Dafydd.

YR Arglwydd *yw* [a] fy Mugail; [b] ni bydd eisiau arnaf.

2 Efe a wna i mi orwedd mewn porfeydd gwelltog: efe a'm tywys ger llaw'r dyfroedd [c] tawel.

3 Efe a ddychwel fy enaid: [d] efe a'm harwain ar hyd llwybrau cyfiawnder er mwyn ei enw.

4 Ie, pe rhodiwn ar hyd glyn [e] cysgod angeu, [f] nid ofnaf niweid: canys *yr wyt* ti gyd â mi; dy wialen a'th ffon a'm cysurant.

5 [g] Ti a arlwyi ford ger fy mron yngŵydd fy ngwrthwynebwyr: [h] iraist fy mhen âg olew: fy phiol sydd lawn.

6 Daioni a thrugaredd yn ddiau a'm canlynant holl ddyddiau fy mywyd: a phreswyliaf yn nhŷ yr Arglwydd [i] yn dragywydd.

In order to demonstrate that interpretation (exegesis) is central to the role of the translator, note the example from the Bible, given below. We must ask ourselves:

"Can a translation be free of interpretation?"
or
"What does the Greek word ἄγγελος mean?"

1. Mark 1:13

οἱ   **ἄγγελοι**   διηκόνουν   αὐτῷ
hoi   angeloi   diēkonoun   autōi
"the _____ were ministering to/serving him"
Question: What does *angeloi* (nominative plural) mean in this context?
Answer: Angels, the supernatural servants of God.

2. Luke 7:24

Ἀπελθόντων   δὲ τῶν   **ἀγγέλων**   Ἰωάννου ...
Apelthontōn   de tōn   angelōn   Iōannou ...
"When the _____ of John had left ..."
Question: What does *angelōn* (genitive plural) mean in this context?
Answer: Human messengers, disciples whom John had sent.

The question naturally arises, how does one know that in Luke 7:24 ἀγγέλων does not mean "supernatural beings"? The answer is clear: we know what ἀγγέλων means in Luke 7:24 not by looking up the word in a Greek dictionary, but only because of the context—the immediate biblical context (Lk. 7:18-20) and the broader biblical context (Heb. 1:13, etc.).

There are two options open to the translator when confronting ἄγγελος in these passages:

1. Consistently translate it by the same word or phrase, or,
2. Translate it at times one way and at times another way, depending upon the context.

Option 1 allows for three possible understandings:

a) John's disciples were supernatural spirit beings.
b) The "legions of angels" (Mt. 26:53), "angels in heaven"/"heavenly angels" (Mk. 13:32, etc.), or "angels of God" (Mt. 22:30) are as human as John's disciples.
c) ἄγγελος means simply "messenger," and whether it is a supernatural spirit-being (Mk. 1:13) or a mere human (Lk. 7:18-19, 24) depends upon interpretation of the context.

But since a and b are clearly false, even very literal translations have wisely followed option 2. In doing so they have interpreted the original. Based upon their interpretations, they have translated ἄγγελος differently according to context. In the case of a certain non-English Bible translation where this was not done, a Christian leader representing that language asked if John the Baptist was in fact an "angel" in the supernatural sense!

From this we can draw several conclusions:

1. It is frequently said that, whereas the *King James Version*, the *New American Standard Version*, or other more literal versions are "translations" and therefore "trustworthy," some other versions are "paraphrases" or "commentaries," full of "interpretations," making them largely "inaccurate."

2. However, as the above example shows, not only does the *KJV* contain "interpretations," no translation can do otherwise.
3. The question is not whether or not to include interpretation in a translation, but to determine to what extent it is necessary, and then to do it consistently and accurately,

in keeping with the meaning of the text and the understanding of the intended audience.

4. It is impossible to always translate literally without being obscure or even absurd.

5. Translation first and foremost is a "carrying over" of meaning, not form. It is not, and can never be, a purely mechanical task.[4]

6. What should be obvious—that all translations contain interpretations—is not always understood. It needs to be emphatically stated. The word ἄγγελος ("messenger") has given us a message.

7. Recognition of the necessity of interpretation in translation need not be the equivalent of unleashing a flood of subjective opinion. Properly understood and applied, it is instead like digging for gold or diamonds. It must be done wisely and carefully, but its neglect relegates the audience to spiritual poverty (cf. 2 Peter 3:16; 2 Timothy 2:15; Proverbs 2:1-6).

5.2 The Bible Itself Gives Examples of Meaning-Based Translation

Mark, the Gospel writer, gives clear witness to the principle of meaning-based translation. In Mark 5:41 he translated Jesus' words—"Talitha koum!" which is Aramaic—into Greek:

> He took her by the hand and said to her, *"Talitha koum!"* (which means, "Little girl, I say to you, get up!").

A more literal translation under the original Greek and Aramaic text[5] looks like this:

καὶ	κρατήσας	τῆς	χειρὸς	τοῦ	παιδίου	λέγει αὐτῇ
and	taking	the	hand	the	of-girl	says to-her

Ταλιθα	κουμ,	ὅ		ἐστιν	μεθερμηνευόμενον
Girl	get-up,	which		is	translated/means

Τὸ	κοράσιον,	σοὶ	λέγω,	ἔγειρε.
—	girl	to-you	I-say	get-up.

Notice carefully the Gospel writer's translation of Jesus' Aramaic. When comparing Christ's two words to Mark's translation of them, we see that Mark added to the Greek both an article (Τὸ) and an entire clause (σοὶ λέγω "I say to you"). Ταλιθα (**Talitha**) means "girl" or "maiden" and κουμ (**koum**) means "get up." So by the evangelist's own account, Jesus never uttered the clause "I say to you." Mark himself added it to his translation! Why? Maybe to avoid a potential misunderstanding in its absence—Jesus was not gruff, but "Girl, get up!" can look that way in print. Or maybe Mark added it to impress upon the reader the majesty and power of

Jesus' words. In any case, we see that it is, in fact, "the thought that counts" (recalling the citation above). Precise thoughts and words gave rise to Mark's precise, but not literal, translation.[6]

This is very significant. While such inclusions are in no way acceptable when approaching translation from a literal point of view, they are often mandatory when holding to a meaning-based approach. Mark's "additions" were required in order to translate the Aramaic into clear, accurate and natural Greek. Mark was not a literalist when approaching translation. For him, clarity and naturalness, without sacrifice of accuracy, were preferable to slavery to a literal theory of translation.[7]

> ¹⁶上帝深深愛世人，甚至連自己的獨生子也賜給他們，叫一切相信祂的，不致滅亡，反得永生。

We can thank God that he is not a literalist, as many would make him out to be. If God were a literalist, very few of us would know anything about the Bible. At best, we would be like many who can "read" (that is, "pronounce") the Koran in Arabic, yet do not understand its meaning.

5.3 The Bible Does Not Teach Literal Translation

Many people around the world ask about Rev. 22:18-19. Doesn't it teach that not a single word should be added or deleted from the book of Revelation, if not God's word as a whole?

> For I testify unto every man that heareth the
> words of the prophecy of this book, If any man
> shall add unto these things, God shall add unto
> him the plagues that are written in this book:
> And if any man shall take away from the words
> of the book of this prophecy, God shall take
> away his part out of the book of life, and out of
> the holy city, and *from* the things which are
> written in this book. (*KJV*)

Clearly, these verses are not to be taken lightly. But what do they really mean? I myself do not take them lightly. I also fear their curse. The following is, I believe, a faithful response:

1. The Greek term λόγος (*logos*), which both the *KJV* and *NIV* render as "words," can sometimes properly be translated that way. But like the situation above regarding the term ἄγγελος, there are many contexts where it is best translated otherwise.

2. The primary meaning of *logos* is not "word" in a grammatical sense—such as "croak," "frog," or "slimy"—but a set of ideas that are intended to be communicated.

3. From its basic definition and New Testament usage, in this  passage *logos* means "truths," "content," or "propositions," not mere "isolated dictionary entries found in the original text." (See, for example, the following passages where *logos* is found: Mt. 19:22; Mk. 5:36; Lk. 1:29; Jn. 2:22; Acts 8:4; Acts 10:29; 2 Pet. 1:19; Gal. 5:14; 1 Tim. 6:3; 2 Tim. 4:15; Rev. 1:2; cf. also Heb. 4:12; Jn. 1:1,14.)

4. Even the translators of the *KJV* acknowledge that by including the word "from" to this very passage (vs. 19, in italics) they have "added" to the word of God. Are they under the curse of Revelation 22 for making their translation more clear and natural than a literal rendering would permit?[8]

5.   The actual meaning of the passage is closer to this: "No one should dare distort (at least willingly, if not out of ignorance) the prophecies in the book of Revelation." Applying that to translation, the case might even be made that an overly literal rendering which obscures their meaning is guilty of "subtracting" from them!

The conclusion is that the principle of Revelation 22:18-19 did not restrict Mark to a literal translation. The same is true for us today. Translators are, nevertheless, still accountable. It is our job to produce an accurate, clear and natural transfer of meaning from the Hebrew, Greek and Aramaic originals to the language of translation.

5.4 The Church Fathers Do Not Teach Literal Translation

For those who put a high value on early Church tradition, the statement by Basil the Great, in a Canonical letter (No. 188) to Amphilochius, may be of interest

I am surprised that you demand literal precision in the [translation of] Scripture, and that you consider the wording to be distorted which sets forth the Scripture's meaning but does not translate exactly what is signified by the Hebrew word.[9]

5.5 For Most Audiences, the Goal is an Accurate, yet Clear and Natural-Sounding Translation.

5.5.1 The Goal of Translation

To obtain the closest equivalence in translation it is necessary to consider three basic requirements: (1) the translation must represent the customary usage of the native language, (2) the translation must make sense, and (3) the translation must conform to the meaning of the original.[10]

In other words, most translations should be:

<u>N</u>atural   (point 1) }
<u>C</u>lear   (point 2) }   "CAN"
<u>A</u>ccurate   (point 3) }

<u>Clarity</u>: The translation is clearly understandable.
<u>Accuracy</u>: The translation accurately reflects the source language meaning.
<u>Naturalness</u>: The translation sounds natural to the receptor language audience.

C + A – N = Stilted, "precise" language that grates on the ear.
C + N – A = Clear communication of the wrong message.
"A" + N – C = No message or the wrong message.

A translation that is "accurate" but does not communicate the proper message is not really accurate at all. (Note the final example, from Acts 2:43, which follows.) If the term "accuracy" is to mean anything, its definition must include reference to reader comprehension.[11] Other descriptions of a good Bible translation might be added, such as "dynamic," "full of impact," "moving," "persuasive," "beautiful," "powerful," etc. But if a translation is truly clear, accurate and naturally worded, it will be powerful and full of impact. God's Word, properly translated, has its own power—the ring of truth (Jn. 17:17), the panorama of eternity (Ecc. 12:12-14), and the ability to penetrate to the core (Heb. 4:12). It needs no embellishment. If

translated in keeping with the above principles, it will have all the life-giving impact with which it was originally imbued. Beyond that, its reception is in large measure dependent upon the "soil" in which it is sown.

5.5.2 Creating a "C.A.N." Translation in Practice

An example based upon Acts 2:43, shown below in Greek-English interlinear form (superscripts represent English word order), illustrates some of the principles used to create a clear, accurate and natural translation in the Higaonon language of the Philippines:

Ἐγίνετο [2] δὲ [1] πάσῃ [4] ψυχῇ [5] φόβος, [3] πολλά [7] τε [6]
There-was[2] now[1] on-every[4] soul[5] fear[3] many[7] and[6]

τέρατα [8] καὶ [9] σημεῖα [10] διὰ [12] τῶν [13] ἀποστόλων [14]
wonders[8] and[9] signs[10] through[12] the[13] apostles[14]

ἐγίνετο (GNT).
were-occurring[11]

A highly literal translation of this verse, taken from the *KJV*, is:

> And fear came upon every soul: and many wonders and signs were done by the apostles.

Now if this verse were translated literally into Higaonon, similar to the way it has been done in the *KJV*, it would be understood by native speakers of the language, but not at all in keeping with the meaning Luke intended. Coming from an animistic background, traditional Higaonons would interpret the passage something like this:

> *A dreadful spirit seized the souls of the people [with resultant dire consequences for their health]; in addition, the apostles [a meaningless term] received power [probably from the same spirit or others like it] to perform many miracles and supernatural signs [which only shamans are believed to do].*

What does a reader understand any particular portion of the Bible to mean? Few would be so bold as to admit it, but for all practical purposes many believe that question to be basically irrelevant. To them, the issue is not what people *do* understand, but what they *should* understand. Why blame a translation if it does not communicate? After all, isn't that what the Holy Spirit is for? Granted, maybe a portion of Scripture should be understood in such and such a way, but the responsibility for good communication does not lie only with the receptor, but also with the communicator. And to the extent that a message is ambiguous, assumes information unknown to the receptor, or employs forms foreign to him or her, to that extent it is inaccessible. Therefore, since we believe that translations are meant to communicate (and not just reproduce the form of the source text), the question of audience comprehension—the reader's understanding—is of utmost importance. In fact, it is so important that we can claim this:

a translation "means" what a consensus of unbiased readers understands it to mean, regardless of what a translator or pastor says it is "supposed" to mean.

Looking again at the Greek original of our example, we see that:

- "soul" means "person."
- "fear" can mean "awe," and in this context almost certainly does.
- "wonders and signs" produced the awe, and therefore were chronologically first.
- καί (*kai*) here does not provide a new topic; "signs" tells more about the "wonders."
- "apostle" is a transliteration from the Greek word meaning "ambassador," "delegate," "messenger" or "envoy."
- It was God who was working through the apostles.

Taking these things into account, the verse was translated like this into Higaonon:

> *And there were many miraculous signs which the envoys performed by means of the power of God in them, and as a result all the people were awestruck.*[12]

To neglect the proper and necessary accommodation to Higaonon language and culture would result in severe miscommunication. If the term *translation* is to mean anything, it must mean anything, it must  include the transfer of meaning.[13] While some places in the Bible are "hard to understand" due to their profound content (2 Pet. 3:16), the terminology and means of expression were generally familiar to typical speakers of the original audience. So it is only fair to ask, don't typical speakers of modern languages deserve access to translations that are equally understandable?

5.5.3 A Notable Quote

Generally speaking, translation is both a science and an art. An excess of either creates distortion. But beyond science and art, especially in the translation of the Bible, there is a third dimension, the spiritual.

It would, of course, be wonderful if satisfactory results in a translations program could be guaranteed merely by laying down valid principles and setting up standard procedures. Such statements of principles and procedures do help, but they will fail utterly unless there are other intangible features which are even more important than these formal rules. These other and more basic ingredients in the work of Bible translating include

1. humility (the essential quality of true scholarship),
2. openness to suggestion,
3. spiritual sensitivity,
4. deep reverence for the message, and
5. an evangelistic spirit, which alone makes possible that degree of empathy with the intended reader so that a truly creative and meaningful translation can be produced.

The real problems of the translation are not technical, they are human; and the ultimate solutions involve the transformation of the human spirit.[14]

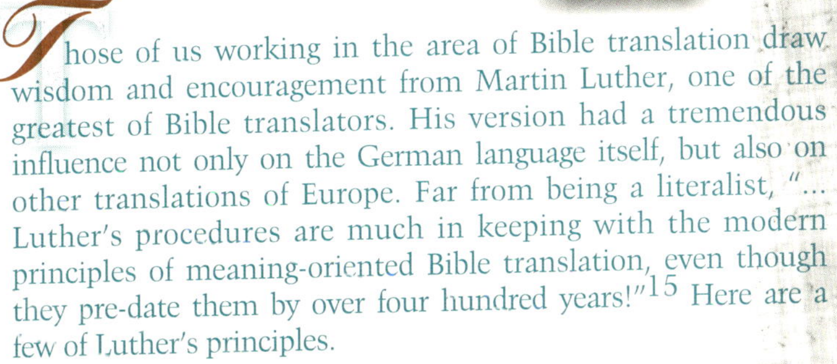

5.5.4 Martin Luther and Bible Translation

Those of us working in the area of Bible translation draw wisdom and encouragement from Martin Luther, one of the greatest of Bible translators. His version had a tremendous influence not only on the German language itself, but also on other translations of Europe. Far from being a literalist, "... Luther's procedures are much in keeping with the modern principles of meaning-oriented Bible translation, even though they pre-date them by over four hundred years!"[15] Here are a few of Luther's principles.

- **It is more important to translate the meaning of the original than to replicate its form.** Luther wrote:

MARTIN LUTHER.

I wanted to speak German, not Latin or Greek, since it was German I had undertaken to speak in the translation ... Therefore I must let the literal words go and try to learn how the German says that which the Hebrew [or Greek] expresses ... [W]ords are to serve and follow the meaning, not meaning the words.[16]

In the preface to Job, Luther writes:

… if it were translated everywhere word for word … and not for the most part according to the sense, no one would understand it. … We have taken care to use language that is clear and that everybody can understand, without perverting the sense and meaning."17

- **There is a corollary to the first principle: In order to communicate, a translation must change the linguistic form of the original.** Luther wrote in reference to Psalm 68:

Whoever would speak German must not use Hebrew style. Rather he must see to it—once he understands the Hebrew author [hence the need for a careful exegesis!]—that he concentrates on the sense of the text, asking himself, 'Pray tell, what do the Germans say in such a situation?' Once he has the German words to serve the purpose, let him drop the Hebrew words and express the meaning freely in the best German he knows.18

- **A translation should reflect the various literary genres in ways which are natural to the receptor language.**

> [Luther's] translation is the German Bible rather than the Bible in German. The German language was like clay in his hands, like a violin played by a virtuoso. The sighs and sobs of some of the Psalms; the high hallelujahs of others; hymns to the God of salvation; the majestic cadences of Isaiah; the lamenting notes of Jeremiah; the profound depth beneath the simple diction of John; the tremendous power of the tense, stormy, telescopic style of Paul—Luther's translation has all of these in German.[19]

- **Translators must maintain close contact with their audience.** Luther states:

> We do not have to inquire of the literal Latin [the language of education and the church in Luther's day –sm], how we are to speak German ... Rather we must inquire about this of the mother in the home, the children on the street, the common man in the marketplace. We must be guided by their language, the way they speak, and do our translating accordingly. That way they will understand it and recognize that we are speaking German to them.[20]

- **The qualities of a good translator are not few.** Luther boldly claims:

> Translation is not an art for anybody, as the misled holy ones think. What is necessary is a fair, devout, faithful, diligent, pious, Christian, learned, well-versed, experienced heart.[21]

- **Finally, Bible translation is possible but not simple.** Luther was one of the most learned men of his age—Doctor of Divinity, polyglot, professor and author. Despite his celebrated qualifications he confessed:

> I have also undertaken to translate the Bible into German. That was necessary for me; otherwise I might have died someday imagining that I was a learned man. Those who think themselves scholars should try to do this work.[22]

Biblia
das ist
Die ganße Heilige
Schrifft
Durch D. Martin Lu-
ther verteutscht.
Mitt Kupfferstücken.
Gedruckt zu Franck-
furt. Inn Verlegung
Matthäi Merian. See-
ligen Erben &c.

ENDNOTES

1 Unless otherwise noted, all English Scripture citations are from the *New International Version*, 1984, Colorado Springs: International Bible Society.

2 Mildred L. Larson, *Meaning-based Translation*, 1984, Lanham, MD: University Press of America, p. 4.

3 Taken from a tract advocating exclusive use of the *King James Version*. In order to prevent embarrassment to its author, the work will not be cited here.

4 For this reason computer-generated translations, while helpful in some situations, are not able to adequately and consistently convey the proper meaning.

5 *The Greek New Testament (GNT)*, Fourth Revised Edition, 1994, Stuttgart: Deutsche Bibelgesellschaft, United Bible Societies.

6 One person objected to this argument, saying that μεθερμηνευό-μενον is not "translated" but "means." In response, by that understanding Mark gave the "meaning" of Christ's words, not the literal "translation," which is precisely the basic tenet of non-literal "functionally equivalent" or "meaning-based" translation.

7 Many New Testament citations of Old Testament passages are not translations of the Hebrew text. Instead, they follow the wording of the Septuagint (the Greek translation of the Old Testament), clearly demonstrating that New Testament authors did not follow a principle of word-for-word adherence to the Hebrew original.

8 There is also a well-known problem with the *KJV's* use of "book of life" in place of the more accurate "tree of life," but that is another story, and a real story at that.

9 Θαυμάζω δέ σου, τὴν γραμματικὴν ἀκρίβειαν ἐπὶ τῆς Γραφῆς ἀπαιτοῦντος, καὶ λογιζομένου ὅτι ἠναγκασμένη ἐστιν ἡ λέξις τῆς ἑρμηνείας τὸ αὐτῆς εὔσημον ἐκδιδούσης, οὐ τὸ κυρίως ὑπὸ τῆς Ἑβραϊκῆς φωνῆς σημαινόμενον μετατιθείσης.

10 Eugene A. Nida, *Bible Translating*, 1947, London: United Bible Societies, p. 13.

11 Exceptions to this might include translations for linguistic purposes (e.g., interlinears, designed to give researchers who do not know the source language insight into its grammar and lexicon), and certain types of legal documents.

12 Daw madakol ha timaan ha mga pugtubad-tubad ha hininang ku mga talawtawan pinaagi ku gahom ku Diyus diyà ta kandan, daw panday on paman nangatoosan su pudu ha mga otaw.

13 The question always remains, of course, how much meaning? The Higaonon text still does not define who "the people" were. That must be gained from the immediate context. Nor does it say anything about the purpose of the miracles. That is left to be pondered.

14 E. A. Nida and and C. R. Taber, *The Theory and Practice of Translation*, 1982, Leiden: E. J. Brill, p. 186.

15 Ernst R. Wendland, "Martin Luther, the Father of Confessional, Functional-Equivalence Bible Translation: Parts 1 and 2" in *Notes on Translation* 9:1 and 9:2 (Dallas: Summer Institute of Linguistics, 1995)
pp. 20-21.

16 Cited in Wendland, p. 23.

17 Ibid., p. 24.

18 Ibid., p. 25.

19 Ewald M. Plass, *This is Luther: A Character Study* (St. Louis: Concordia, 1948), p. 36, cited in Wendland, p. 33.

20 Cited in Wendland, p. 26.

21 E. Arndt, ed., Martin Luther. Sendbrief vom Dolmetschen und Summarien über die Psalmen und Ursachen des Dolmetschens. Mit einem Anhang ausgewählter Selbstzeugnisse und Übersetzungsproben (Halle/Saale: Max Niemeyer Verlag, 1968), cited in Charles Atangana Nama, et al., "Translators and the Development of National Languages" in Translators Through History, Jean Delisle and Judith Woodsworth, eds. (Philadelphia: John Benjamins, 1995) p. 37.

22 Martin Luther, "A Letter of Consolation to All who Suffer Persecution Because of God's Word, Addressed to Hartmut von Cronberg," *Luther's Works, AE*, vol 43, Devotional Writings: II, Gustav K. Wiencke, ed., Helmut T. Lehmann, gen. ed. (Philadelphia: Fortress Press) p. 70.

DESCRIPTION OF ILLUSTRATIONS

Cover: *The Tower of Babel*, adapted from an engraving by Gustave Doré.

Edging: Egyptian papyrus, the "paper" used in many early Biblical manuscripts.

Page 1:   *The Tower of Babel*, from a 1545 Luther Bible.

Page 1:   *The Lamb before the Throne*, Revelation chapters 4-5, from a 1545 Luther Bible.

Page 2:   Map of *The Holie Land*, from a 1582 edition of the English language *Geneva Bible*, a predecessor of the *King James Version*.

Page 3:   An unnamed artist's depiction of ancient scribes.

Page 4:   Celtic cross.

Page 5:   Ancient Grecian architecture.

Page 6:   Abbreviated form of the 10 Commandments in Hebrew.

Page 7:   Cover page of a 1529 edition of the Latin *Vulgate* Bible. (Note the stamp in the lower right corner, which reads "SOC. JESU.," the Society of Jesus [Jesuits]).

Page 8:   Kremlin Cathedral, Moscow.

Page 8:   Classroom scene, Russia.

Page 9:   Traditional Kazahk yurt, USSR.

Page 9:   Soviet "babushka."

Page 9:   St. Basil's Cathedral, Moscow.

Page 10:   Table of contents from an edition of the 1611 *King James (Authorized) Version*. Note the inclusion of *The Bookes called Apocrypha*.

Page 11:   Psalm 23 from an old, undated edition of the Welsh Bible.

Page 11:   Ancient stone marker, Etchmiadzin/Ejmiastin, Armenia, the first nation to officially embrace Christianity.

Page 12:   Egyptian pyramids.

Page 12:   Art from India.

Page 13:   From the title page of a 1595 edition of the English language *Bishops' Bible*, a predecessor of the *King James Version*.

Page 14:   The "mighty angel" of Revelation 10, from a 1545 Luther Bible.

Page 15:   Man from the Middle East.